From: Peggy
Sent: Friday, March 18, 2011
To: Alex; Mary; Dan; Kate
Subject: FW: Amazing Saying

This is awesome!

Inspiring Message

...ing in there!

Favorite Quotes and Sayings,

Words of Inspiration

and

Encouragement

From: Forwarded E-mails

From: Moia
Sent: Saturday, February 5, 2011
To: Carolyn; Patty; Andrea
Subject: FW: Great Quote

This is one to keep!

From: Carolyn
Sent: Sunday, January 9, 2011
To: Art
Subject: FW: Just Received This

Made me think of you!

Favorite Quotes and Sayings,

Words of Inspiration

and

Encouragement

From: Forwarded E-mails

Carolyn B Bellanca

iUniverse, Inc.
Bloomington

Favorite Quotes and Sayings, Words of Inspiration and Encouragement From: Forwarded E-mails

iUniverse books may be ordered through booksellers or by contacting:

iUniverse
1663 Liberty Drive
Bloomington, IN 47403
www.iuniverse.com
1-800-Authors (1-800-288-4677)

ISBN: 978-1-4620-4264-7 (sc)
ISBN: 978-1-4620-4265-4 (ebk)

Printed in the United States of America

iUniverse rev. date: 08/11/2011

For my sons.

Introduction

I've been saving quotes and sayings for so many years I've lost count. My collection is now probably four times what is here. These are my absolute favorites though, received via email, from friends, family and people I have worked with. These are the ones that get me to move or keep me going, and since I have also heard several of them used by others in speeches, sermons, in movies and on television, they seem to be favorites of many. I thought why not have them all in one place, easily accessible, whenever someone needs a little inspiration and encouragement.

Life Lessons

The first quote in this section is the first one I saved. It reflects my basic philosophy on life: accept responsibility for your actions but try everything, take chances, go places you've never been, meet people from all over the world, try to take advantage of every opportunity that comes your way, and most of all never throw in the towel. It's okay to make mistakes-that's how you learn. This is what I want to pass on to my boys. I feel the quotes and sayings in "Life Lessons" all speak to this, which is probably why I love them so much and why they have had such a powerful effect on my life.

Life is a great big canvas; throw
all the paint on it you can.
Danny Kaye

Think. Believe. Dream. Dare.
Credo of Walt Disney

For of all sad words of tongue and pen, the saddest are these, "It might have been".
John Greenleaf Whittier

Constantly choosing the lesser of two evils is still choosing evil.
Jerry Garcia

Experience is a hard teacher because she
gives the test first, the lesson afterwards.
Vernon Sanders Law

Experience is a wonderful thing. It enables you to
recognize a mistake when you make it again.
Anonymous

In the end what we regret the most are the
chances we never took.
Frasier Crane

It's hard to beat a person
who never gives up.
Babe Ruth

You miss 100% of the shots you don't take.
Wayne Gretzky

We seldom think of what we have,
but always think of what we miss.
Anonymous

The best things in life aren't things.
Anonymous

Finish every day and be done with it. You have done what you could. Some blunders and absurdities no doubt crept in; but get rid of them and forget them as soon as you can. Tomorrow is a new day, and you should never encumber its potentialities and invitation with the dread of the past. You should not waste a moment of today on the rottenness of yesterday.
Ralph Waldo Emerson

What you do speaks so loud that
I cannot hear what you say.
Ralph Waldo Emerson

Never borrow from the future. If you worry about what may happen tomorrow and it doesn't happen, you have worried in vain. Even if it does happen, you have to worry twice.
Anonymous

Plan for tomorrow, but live for today.
Anonymous

Birthdays are good for you.
The more you have,
the longer you live.
Anonymous

Happiness is a choice.
Anonymous

We could learn a lot from crayons. Some are sharp, some are pretty and some are dull. Some have weird names, and all are different colors, but they all have to live in the same box.
Anonymous

Differences only weaken us
when they divide us.
Archie Griffin

Be kind, for everyone you meet
is fighting a hard battle.
Plato

Don't cry because it's over,
smile because it happened.
Theodore Seuss Geisel "Dr. Seuss"

Be who you are and say what you feel,
because those who mind don't matter
and those who matter don't mind.
Dr. Seuss

It is not good to compare yourself to others.
Anonymous

Always remember that you're unique.
Just like everyone else.
Anonymous

The world is round and the place which may seem
like the end may also be only the beginning.
Ivy Baker Priest

Don't worry about the world coming to an end
today. It's already tomorrow in Australia.
Charles Schultz

As we express our gratitude, we must never forget
that the highest appreciation is not to utter words,
but to live by them.
John F. Kennedy

We can't help everyone, but
everyone can help someone.
Ronald Reagan

Courage is almost a contradiction in terms.
It means a strong desire to live taking the
form of readiness to die.
G.K. Chesterton

Freedom is never free.
Anonymous

The greatest test of courage on earth
is to bear defeat without losing heart.
Robert G. Ingersoll

Life happens when you're busy making other plans.
John Lennon

Reality leaves a lot to the imagination.
John Lennon

Junk is something you've kept for years and
throw away two weeks before you need it.
Edward A Murphy

He who dies with the most toys is still dead.
Anonymous

If you tell the truth, you don't
have to remember anything.
Mark Twain

It's not the size of the dog in the fight,
but the size of the fight in the dog.
Mark Twain

Two people can look at the same
thing and see it differently.
Anonymous

What we see depends mainly
on what we look for.
Sir John Lubbock

It's never too late to be what
you might have been.
George Eliot

Determine <u>what</u> is to blame,
not <u>who</u> is to blame.
Anonymous

The measure of a life, after all, is
not its duration, but its donation.
Corrie ten Boom

Worry is a cycle of inefficient thoughts
whirling around a center of fear.
Corrie ten Boom

Worry does not empty tomorrow of its
sorrow; it empties today of its strength.
Corrie ten Boom

Luck is where opportunity meets preparation.
Seneca

> If one does not know to which port
> one is sailing, no wind is favourable.
> *Seneca*
> *(In other words: If you don't know where*
> *you are going, you will never get there.)*

The happy man is content with his present lot,
no matter what it is, and is reconciled to his
circumstances.
Seneca

Everyone is kneaded out of the same dough
but not baked in the same oven.
Yiddish Proverb

When you hear something, you will forget it.
When you see something, you will remember it.
But not until you do something, will you understand it.
Old Chinese Proverb

It ain't braggin' if you can back it up.
Dizzy Dean

A woman is like a tea bag-you never know
how strong she is until she gets in hot water.
Eleanor Roosevelt

Flatter me, and I may not believe you.
Criticize me, and I may not like you.
Ignore me, and I may not forgive you.
Encourage me, and I may not forget you.
Sir William Arthur

The space between ideals and reality
is filled with a lot of hard work.
Anonymous

Laughter is like changing a baby's diaper.
It doesn't permanently solve any problems,
but it makes things more acceptable for a while.
Anonymous

My idea of housework is to sweep
the room with a glance.
Anonymous

We make a Living by what we get,
but we make a Life by what we give.
Sir Winston Churchill

No one cares what you know
until they know that you care.
Anonymous

The only place where your dream becomes
impossible is in your own mind.
Dr. Robert Schuller

Press on. Obstacles are seldom the
same size tomorrow as they are today.
Dr. Robert Schuller

Tough times never last, but
tough people do.
Dr. Robert Schuller

Life is not measured by the number of breaths we take,
but by the moments that take our breath away.
Anonymous

Lose an hour in the morning, and you
will spend all day looking for it.
Richard Whately

Wherever you are, be all there.
Jim Elliot

If not now then when? If not me then who?
Hillel

A person who flies into a rage
seldom makes a good landing.
Walt Whitman

A closed mouth gathers no feet.
Anonymous

The best way to predict the future
is to help create it.
Anonymous

Pay attention and learn from other people's
mistakes, because you'll never live long
enough to make them all yourself.
Anonymous

No one crosses a river without getting wet.
Anonymous

It is easier to get forgiveness than permission.
Stuart's Law of Retroaction

Insanity: doing the same thing over and
over again and expecting different results.
Albert Einstein

A person who has never made a mistake
has never tried anything new.
Albert Einstein

Great spirits have always encountered
opposition from mediocre minds.
Albert Einstein

Character cannot be developed in ease and quiet.
Only through experience of trial and suffering can
the soul be strengthened, ambition inspired,
and success achieved.
Helen Keller

Life can only be understood backwards;
but it must be lived forward.
Soren Kierkegaard

Absolute weight doesn't matter. It depends on how long you try to hold it. Holding a raised glass for a minute isn't a problem. If you hold it for an hour you'll have an ache in your arm. If you hold it for a day, you'll have to call an ambulance. In each case it's the same weight, but the longer you hold it, the heavier it becomes. The same is true for burdens. If we carry our burdens all the time, sooner or later, we won't be able to carry on. As with the water, you have to put it down for a while and rest before holding it again. So, before you return home each night, put the burden of work down. Don't carry it home. You can pick it up again tomorrow. Life is short. Enjoy it!

Anonymous

Additional Reader Favorite Quotes & Sayings

We moved every couple of years while I was growing up, which helped instill in me a sense of adventure and willingness to try new things. As a result, I have lived in 9 states and 3 countries, and been to 45 states (including Alaska and Hawaii) and 20 countries (including Russia, East Germany and Czechoslovakia before the wall came down). At the time of this picture at Yosemite we lived in Northern California. On our move there, we were passing right by the Grand Canyon and my Dad didn't want to stop, thinking we'd be back by there again sometime. I convinced him to stop, which was good, because we never have gotten back there again as a family.

Carolyn Bickford
Summer 1979
Americans Abroad AFS Student to
Berne   Switzerland

Photo/Courtesy of Coronet Studies

I spent the summer after graduation from high school in Berne, Switzerland as an AFS Exchange student. It was an honor to be chosen and was such a great experience. Before I had even left the States, I had met a couple hundred American kids from all over the country. My Swiss host family was wonderful and showed me so much, however, since I had only taken French and Berne is in the German speaking part of the country, we had to speak English. I decided then to learn German, so I could go back in college (which I did my Junior year).

I spent my Junior year of college abroad, near Nuremberg, Germany, through the University of Kansas. I was the first business student in the program. We lived in the foreign students dorm, which housed many German students too. I saw and learned so much that year. Many friendships were forged with people from all over the world. Barriers were broken and stereotypes were smashed as a result. I think there would be a lot less trouble in the world if everyone had an opportunity to do this at some point in their lives. This picture was taken on a trip to Prague, Czechoslovakia.

I had a railpass and used it every chance I got. A friend and I traveled for a month all over Europe between semesters. We would wake up in the morning and decide where we wanted to go next. We saw every place I'd ever dreamt of seeing. On a separate trip we even went to Moscow and Leningrad (now St. Petersberg again).

Faith, Family and Friendship

The quotes and sayings in this section, I feel help inspire the strength and extra confidence needed to strike out and do the things you've never done before, while at the same time still helping to keep you grounded in truth and values, so you don't end up going down the wrong path. I have learned over the years that I really don't have much control over what happens in my life (other than my own actions), but that doesn't mean that I can just go through life as a bystander. At the end of every situation if I can say to myself "I did everything I could do", I am satisfied. I think these quotes and sayings in "Faith, Family and Friendship" have helped me do that.

You must be the change you
wish to see in the world.
Mahatma Gandhi

When I despair, I remember that all through history
the ways of truth and love have always won.
There have been tyrants, and murderers,
and for a time they can seem invincible,
but in the end they always fall.
Think of it . . . always.
Mahatma Gandhi

The Golden Rule is a general moral principle found in virtually all religions and cultures: "Love your neighbor as yourself "(*Moses*); "Do unto others as you would have them do to you" popularly rephrased as "Treat others as you want to be treated" (*Jesus*); "What you do not want others to do to you, do not do to others" (*Confucius*); "What is hateful to you, do not to your fellow man" (*Jewish sage Hillel*)

> All that we are is a result of what we
> have thought. The mind is everything.
> What we think, we become.
> *Buddha*

Each morning as you wake, there is a new opportunity . . .
God does not tell you what He is going to do next . . .
A life of faith is not a life of one glorious mountain top
experience after another, but it is a life of day-in and
day-out consistency, a life of walking without fainting.
Living a life of faith means never knowing where
you are being led. But it does mean knowing
the One who is leading.
Oswald Chambers

When it is a question of God's
Almighty Spirit, never say "I can't".
Oswald Chambers

What good is it to gain the whole
world and yet forfeit your soul.
Mark 8:36

Open arms to change, but
don't let go of your values.
Dalai Lama

Praise be to the God and Father of our Lord Jesus Christ,
the Father of compassion and the God of all comfort,
who comforts us in all our troubles, so that we can
comfort those in any trouble with the comfort we
ourselves have received from God.
2 Corinthians 1:3-4

For God so loved the world,
that he gave his only Son,
that whoever believes in Him
should not perish but have
eternal life. For God did not
send his Son into the world to
condemn the world, but in order
that the world might be
saved through Him.
John 3:16-17

When there is nothing left but God, that is
when you find out that God is all you need.
Anonymous

Before God we are all equally
wise—and equally foolish.
Albert Einstein

This will be a better world when the power
of love replaces the love of power!
Anonymous

The glory of friendship is not the outstretched hand,
nor the kindly smile, nor the joy of companionship;
it is the spiritual inspiration that comes to one
when he discovers that someone else believes
in him and is willing to trust him.
Ralph Waldo Emerson

All mothers are working mothers.
Anonymous

All great change in America
begins at the dinner table.
Ronald Reagan

God always gives His best to those
who leave the choice with Him.
Jim Elliot

Therefore, do not worry about tomorrow,
for tomorrow will worry about itself. Each
day has enough trouble of its own.
Matthew 6:34

You must do whatever you say you will do.
Deuteronomy 23:23

Life takes its own turns, makes its own demands,
writes its own story, and along the way, we start to
realize we are not the author. We begin to understand
that life is ours to live but not to waste and that the
greatest rewards are found in the commitments we
make with our whole hearts-to the people we love
and to the causes that earn our sacrifice.
George W. Bush

Faith gives us conscience to keep us honest,
even when nobody else is looking.
George W. Bush

The deeper the roots, the higher the reach.
Anonymous

Be true to yourself. At the end of the day,
you're the only person who has to like you.
Anonymous

Live a good, honorable life. Then when
you get older and think back, you'll be
able to enjoy it a second time.
Dalai Lama

Follow the three R's: Respect for self,
Respect for others, and
Responsibility for all your actions.
Dalai Lama

Remember that not getting what you want
is sometimes a wonderful stroke of luck.
Dalai Lama

Spend some time alone every day,
and once a year, go someplace
you've never been before.
Dalai Lama

Celebrate what's **right** in the world!
Anonymous

Happiness keeps you sweet,
trials keep you strong,
sorrows keep you human,
failures keep you humble,
success keeps you glowing,
but only God keeps you going!
Anonymous

Father, God bless all my friends in whatever it is
that You know they may need *this* day! And may
their lives be full of Your peace, prosperity, and
power as they seek to have a closer relationship
with You. In Jesus' name. Amen
Anonymous

When things don't turn out the way they should,
if you have faith, you just need to trust that
every outcome is always to your advantage.
You just might not know it until some time later.
Anonymous

Faith makes things possible . . . not easy.
Anonymous

Sometimes we are so busy adding up our troubles
that we forget to count our blessings.
Anonymous

Just because someone doesn't love you the
way you want them to, doesn't mean they
don't love you with all they have.
Anonymous

Maybe God wants us to meet a few wrong
people before meeting the right one, so
that when we finally meet the person,
we will know how to be grateful.
Anonymous

As we grow up, we learn that even the one person that wasn't supposed to ever let you down probably will. You will have your heart broken probably more than once and it's harder every time. You'll break hearts too, so remember how it felt when yours was broken. You'll fight with your best friend. You'll blame a new love for things an old one did. You'll cry because time is passing too fast, and you'll eventually lose someone you love. So take too many pictures, laugh too much, and love like you've never been hurt because every sixty seconds you spend upset is a minute of happiness you'll never get back. Don't be afraid that your life will end, be afraid that it will never begin.

Anonymous

Dogs have owners, cats have staff.
Anonymous

I figure if the kids are alive at the end
of the day, I've done my job.
Roseanne

Happy moments, Praise God;
Difficult moments, Seek God;
Quiet moments, Worship God;
Painful moments, Trust God;
Every moment, Thank God.
Anonymous

God grant me the serenity to accept the
things I cannot change, the courage
to change the things I can, and the
wisdom to know the difference.
The Serenity Prayer

Be strong and courageous!
Do not be afraid or discouraged,
for the Lord your God is with you
wherever you go.
Joshua 1:9

Create in me a clean heart, O God, and renew a
right spirit within me. Cast me not away from your
presence, and take not your Holy Spirit from me.
Restore to me the joy of your salvation,
and uphold me with a willing spirit.
Psalm 51: 10-12

May today there be peace within. May you trust your highest power that you are exactly where you are meant to be. May you not forget the infinite possibilities that are born of faith. May you use those gifts that you have received, and pass on the love that has been given to you. May you be content knowing you are a child of God. Let this presence settle into your bones, and allow your soul the freedom to sing and dance. It is there for each and every one of you.

Anonymous

Going to church doesn't make you a Christian any
more than standing in your garage makes you a car.
Anonymous

A day hemmed with prayer is
less likely to unravel.
Anonymous

Love doesn't make the world go round.
Love is what makes the ride worthwhile.
Franklin P. Jones

God throws our sins into the depths of the sea and
then he posts a sign saying "No fishing allowed".
Corrie ten Boom

Never be afraid to trust an unknown
future to a known God.
Corrie ten Boom

Faith sees the invisible, believes the unbelievable,
and receives the impossible.
Corrie ten Boom

Any concern too small to be turned into prayer
is too small to be made into a burden.
Corrie ten Boom

Everybody can be great . . . because anybody can serve.
You don't have to have a college degree to serve.
You don't have to make your subject and verb agree to serve.
You only need a heart full of grace.
A soul generated by love.
Martin Luther King Jr.

Darkness cannot drive out darkness; only
light can do that. Hate cannot drive
out hate; only love can do that.
Martin Luther King Jr.

Cleaning your house while your kids are still growing
is like shoveling the walk before it stops snowing.
Phyllis Diller

Insanity is hereditary; you
get it from your children.
Sam Levenson

Our deepest fear is not that we are inadequate. Our deepest fear is that we are powerful beyond measure. It is our light, not our darkness, that most frightens us. We ask ourselves, who am I to be brilliant, gorgeous, talented and fabulous. Actually, who are you not to be? You are a child of God. Your playing small doesn't serve the world. There's nothing enlightened about shrinking so that other people won't feel insecure around you. We were born to make manifest the glory of God that is within us. It's not just in some of us-it's in everyone. And as we let our own light shine, we unconsciously give other people permission to do the same. As we are liberated from our own fear, our presence automatically liberates others.

Marianne Williamson

To forgive is to set a prisoner free and to
discover that the prisoner was you.
Lewis Smedes

It is not enough to forgive others;
you also need to forgive yourself.
Anonymous

Anyone can count the number of seeds in an apple,
but only God can count the number of apples in a seed.
Dr. Robert Schuller

It is difficult to say what is impossible,
for the dream of yesterday
is the hope of today
and the reality of tomorrow.
Dr. Robert Schuller

I am . . . I can . . . I will.
Dr. Robert Schuller

A professor stood before his philosophy class and had some items in front of him. He picked up a very large mayonnaise jar and filled it with golf balls, then pebbles, sand and two cups of coffee. After each he asked if the jar was now filled, to which the students responded yes each time and were surprised that more would fit in the jar. "Now, said the professor, "I want you to recognize that this jar represents your life. The golf balls are the important things-your God, family, your children, your health, your friends, and your favorite passions-things that if everything else was lost and only they remained your life would still be full. The pebbles are the other things that matter like your job, your house, and your car. The sand is everything else-the small stuff. If you put the sand into the jar first, there is no room for the pebbles or the golf balls. The same goes for life. If you spend all your time and energy on the small stuff, you will never have room for the things that are important to you. Take care of the golf balls first-the things that really matter. Set your priorities. The rest is just sand." One of the students inquired what the coffee represented. The professor smiled. "I'm glad you asked. It just goes to show you that no matter how full your life may seem, there's always room for a couple of cups of coffee with a friend."

Anonymous

Additional Reader Favorite Quotes & Sayings

This has always been one of my favorite pictures of my older son when he was around 2 years old. This picture helps remind me to enjoy the simple pleasures in life and to always try to live in the moment.

Our first cruise was to the Eastern Caribbean, with friends from California (we were living in Ohio by then). I've thought ever since that working on a cruise ship would be a great first job for my boys when they were just out of school. Travel, learn to work really hard and meet people from all over the world. Much like an exchange program, but better. They pay you!

In 2010 my parents celebrated their 50th Wedding Anniversary. We all celebrated on a cruise to Alaska!

Who doesn't at least wonder about the existence of God, when you see a beautiful sunset like this?

Achievement

I believe the quotes and sayings in this section emphasize that sure, you won't win every time, but you have to set out striving to win or it won't ever happen. Achievement doesn't just happen, it requires commitment and effort and follow through. It also requires a willingness to take chances, to work hard, to make mistakes and to never, never give up. I ended "Achievement" with my favorite saying in the book as it is the most important message I wanted to convey. The message: Perseverance is so extremely important if you want to succeed at anything in life.

Aim high and consider yourself
capable of great things.
Elbert Hubbard

To avoid criticism: do nothing,
say nothing, be nothing.
Elbert Hubbard

The greatest mistake you can make is to
be continually fearing you will make one.
Elbert Hubbarb

Success is not found in what you have achieved
but rather in who you have become.
Zen Expression

Self-conquest is the greatest of all victories.
Plato

Success is getting what you want;
Happiness is wanting what you get.
Dale Carnegie

Failure is the opportunity to begin again more
intelligiently.
Henry Ford

Whether you think you can, or
you can't, you are probably right.
Henry Ford

You can't build a reputation on what
you are going to do.
Henry Ford

We do what we know how to do, and
when we know better, we do better.
Maya Angelou

> Excellence is to do a common
> thing in an uncommon way.
> *Booker T. Washington*

The best way to make your dreams
come true is to wake up.
Muhammed Ali

Hard work spotlights the character of people:
some turn up their sleeves, some turn up
their noses, and some don't turn up at all.
Sam Ewing

The reason many people do not recognize
opportunity when it knocks is that it is
usually disguised as hard work.
Anonymous

Winners make things happen;
losers let things happen.
Anonymous

COMMITMENT: Commitment is a line you
cross . . . it's the difference between dreaming
and doing.
Bernie Fuchs

EFFORT: For every person who climbs
the ladder of success . . . there are a
dozen waiting for an elevator.
K. Griffith

CHANGE: The road to success is always
under construction.
Anonymous

CHALLENGES: Little minds are
tamed and subdued by misfortune,
but great minds rise above them.
Washington Irving

The great inspire others through
motivation, not intimidation.
Anonymous

Don't try so hard, the best things come
when you least expect them to.
Anonymous

Don't be irreplaceable. If you can't be
replaced, you can't be promoted.
Anonymous

Winning starts with beginning.
Dr. Robert Schuller

Spectacular achievement is always preceded
by unspectacular preparation.
Dr. Robert Schuller

I'd rather attempt to do something great and fail
than to attempt to do nothing and succeed.
Dr. Robert Schuller

God helps those who help themselves.
Benjamin Franklin

You will find the key to success
under the alarm clock.
Benjamin Franklin

Many of life's failures are people who did not
realize how close they were to success
when they gave up.
Thomas Edison

We build the ladder by which we rise.
Daniel Webster

The world is an astounding place.
Amazing things can happen
when you open your mind
to new possibilities.
Anonymous

Never be afraid to try something new.
Remember, amateurs built the ark;
professionals built the Titanic!
Anonymous

Ladder of Achievement
(Chance of Success)

100%-I Did
90%-I Will
80%-I Can
70%-I Think I Can
60%-I Might
50%-I Think I Might
40%-What Is It?
30%-I Wish I Could
20%-I Don't Know How
10%-I Can't
0%-I Won't

Anonymous

Nobody can make you feel inferior
without your permission.
Eleanor Roosevelt

Let your efforts rise above your excuses.
Anonymous

An error doesn't become a mistake
until you refuse to correct it.
Orlando Battista

Opportunities always look bigger
going than coming.
Anonymous

Great opportunities are often disguised
as unsolvable problems.
Anonymous

Every noble work seems at first impossible.
Anonymous

Success:
To laugh often and much;
to win the respect of intelligent people
and the affection of children;
to earn the appreciation of honest critics
and endure the betrayal of false friends;
to appreciate beauty; to find the best in others;
to leave the world a bit better,
whether by a healthy child,
a garden patch
or a redeemed social condition;
to know even one life has breathed easier
because you have lived.
This is to have succeeded.

Ralph Waldo Emerson

Property is the fruit of labor; property is desirable;
it is a positive good in the world. That some should be
rich shows that others may become rich, and hence,
is just another encouragement to industry and enterprise.
Abraham Lincoln

You cannot help the poor by destroying the rich.
You cannot strengthen the weak by weakening the strong.
You cannot bring about prosperity by discouraging thrift.
You cannot lift the wage earner up by pulling the wage payer down.
You cannot further the brotherhood of man by inciting class hatred.
You cannot build character and courage by taking
away people's initiative and independence.
You cannot help people permanently by doing for them,
what they could and should do for themselves.
Abraham Lincoln

There are three keys to success:
1) Being at the right place at the right time,
2) Knowing you are there,
3) Taking action.
Ray Kroc

He who would like to have something he never
had, will have to do something well,
that he hasn't done yet.
Anonymous

Be not afraid of greatness. Some are born
great. Some achieve greatness. Some
have greatness thrust upon them.
William Shakespeare, "Twelfth Night"

We are what we repeatedly do. Excellence
then is not an act but a habit.
Aristotle

Whatever the mind can conceive
and believe, it can achieve.
Napolean Hill

Sow a thought, reap an action;
sow an action, reap a habit;
sow a habit, reap a character;
sow a character, reap a destiny.
Ralph Waldo Emerson

A winner is someone who recognizes his
God given talents . . . works his tail off to
develop them into skills . . . and uses these
skills to accomplish his goals.
Larry Bird

Find a way, 'cause that's what winners do.
Big Z, "Surf's Up"

We usually learn more from our
mistakes than our victories.
Archie Griffin

God didn't put us on this earth to be ordinary.
Lou Holtz

If A equals success, then the formula is: A
equals X plus Y and Z, with X being work,
Y play, and Z keeping your mouth shut.
Albert Einstein

Logic will get you from A to B.
Imagination will take you anywhere.
Albert Einstein

Try not to become a man of success but
rather to become a man of value.
Albert Einstein

The important thing is not to stop questioning.
Albert Einstein

If you learn from defeat, you haven't really lost.
Zig Ziglar

A goal properly set is halfway reached.
Zig Ziglar

It was character that got us out of bed,
commitment that moved us into action, and
discipline that enabled us to follow through.
Zig Ziglar

It must be remembered that the purpose of education
is not to fill the minds of students with facts . . .
it is to teach them to think, if that is possible,
and always to think for themselves.
Robert M. Hutchins

Education's purpose is to replace
an empty mind with an open one.
Malcolm Forbes

Whether we learn differently or not,
that does not mean you don't have
greatness inside of you.
Henry Winkler

Lazy hands make a man poor, but
diligent hands bring wealth.
Proverbs 10:4

All jobs are easy to the person
who doesn't have to do them.
Holt's Law

Obsessed is how the lazy
describe the dedicated.
Anonymous

Generally speaking, you aren't learning
much when your lips are moving.
Anonymous

The quickest way to double your money is to
fold it in half and put it back in your pocket.
Will Rogers

Even if you're on the right track, you'll
still get run over if you just sit there.
Will Rogers

Experience is something you don't
get until just after you need it.
Anonymous

It is impossible for anyone to learn that
which he thinks he already knows.
Plutarch's Rule

It's what you do when you don't have
to that determines what you will
be when you can't help it.
Anonymous

People with a positive attitude:
focus on the good rather than the bad;
use positive language;
naturally give compliments;
understand that mistakes are normal
and try to learn from them;
have dreams and goals for the future.
Anonymous

> Those who cannot remember the
> past are condemned to repeat it.
> *George Santayana*

When one door closes another door opens;
but we often look so long and so regretfully
upon the closed door that we do not see
the ones which open for us.
Alexander Graham Bell

Our lives improve only when we take
chances—and the first and most difficult risk
we can take is to be honest with ourselves.
Walter Anderson

Only those who will risk going too far can
possibly find out how far one can go.
T.S. Eliot

An idealist believes the short run doesn't count.
A cynic believes the long run doesn't matter.
A realist believes that what is done or left undone
in the short run determines the long run.
Sydney J. Harris

When you lose, don't lose the lesson.
Dalai Lama

Judge your success by what you
had to give up in order to get it.
Dalai Lama

Remember that great love and great
achievements involve great risk.
Dalai Lama

Do or do not. There is no try.
Yoda

Whatever you can do or dream you can,
begin it. Boldness has genius, power,
and magic in it. Begin it now.
Goethe

Anything's possible if you've got enough nerve.
J.K. Rowling

When things go wrong as they sometimes will, and the road you are trudging seems all uphill; when the funds are low and the debts are high, and you want to smile but you have to sigh; when care is pressing you down a bit, rest if you must but DON'T YOU QUIT! For life is strange with its twists and turns, as every one of us sometimes learns; but many a coward turns about when he might have won had he stuck it out, but he learns too late when the night comes down how close he was to the golden crown. Victory is defeat turned inside out. The silver tint of the clouds of doubt. You will never know how near you are . . . it may be close when it seems afar. So stick to the fight when you are hardest hit. It is when things seem worst that YOU MUST NOT QUIT!

Anonymous

Additional Reader Favorite Quotes & Sayings

My father grew up on a farm, close to the Canadian (Quebec) border in Vermont, with eight brothers and sisters. It was a tough life which helped to form in him an amazing work ethic, which thankfully he was able to pass on to my sisters and me. My mother also passed on to us a wonderful work ethic along with another very important trait, the selfless giving of ourselves to others.

I graduated from the University of Missouri, Columbia in 1983, with a Bachelor of Science Degree in Business Administration. At the time my father was Chairman of another department there. It was a solid foundation, but didn't mean life would be easy. I have had to start over five times in my professional life. Throw being a wife and mother into the mix and it's been constant turmoil, but worth it. I wouldn't change a thing.

This was my younger son's graduation from Pre-School. So much to look forward to. He tends to jump in with both feet in everything he does, just like his Mom!

I find myself often awestruck by the beauty of a particular moment. It doesn't matter what else I may be dealing with at the time. At that moment, life couldn't be any better.